Virtual Apprentice

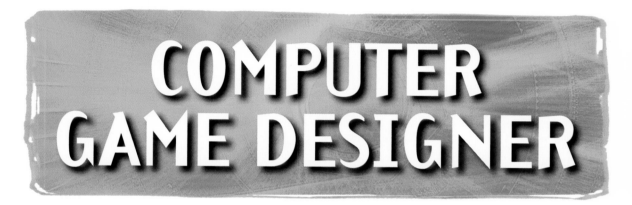

COMPUTER GAME DESIGNER

By Don Rauf
and Monique Vescia

Ferguson
An imprint of Infobase Publishing

Virtual Apprentice: Computer Game Designer

Ferguson
An imprint of Infobase Publishing
132 West 31st Street
New York, NY 10001

ISBN-10: 0-8160-6754-6
ISBN-13: 978-0-8160-6754-1

Library of Congress Cataloging-in-Publication Data

Rauf, Don.
  Virtual apprentice : computer game designer / Don Rauf and Monique Vescia.
    p. cm.
  Includes index.
  ISBN 978-0-8160-6754-1 (hc : alk. paper) 1. Computer games – Programming. 2. Computer games – Programming – Vocational guidance. 3. Electronic games industry – United States.
  I. Vescia, Monique. II. Title.
  QA76.76.C672R39 2007
  794.8'1526--dc22

                      2006036565

Ferguson books are available at special discounts when purchased in bulk quantities for businesses, associations, institutions, or sales promotions. Please call our Special Sales Department in New York at (212) 967-8800 or (800) 322-8755.

You can find Ferguson on the World Wide Web at http://www.fergpubco.com

Produced by Bright Futures Press (http://www.brightfuturespress.com)
Series created by Diane Lindsey Reeves
Interior design by Tom Carling, carlingdesign.com
Cover design by Salvatore Luongo

Photo Credits: Table of Contents Vaughn Youtz/ZUMA/Corbis; Page 5 Tomasz Trogranowski; Page 7 Jaimie Duplass; Page 8 Audrey Armvagov; Page 10 Ralf-Finn Hestoft/Corbis; Page 15 Jacob Wackerhuasen; Page 16 JupiterImages; Page 23 phdpsx; Page 24 Jamie Cross; Page 27 Floris Leeuwenberg/The Cover Story/Corbis; Page 31 Florea Marius Catalin; Page 32 Lee Morris; Page 34 Vaughn Youtz/ZUMA/Corbis; Page 36 Serge Krouglikoff/zefa/Corbis; Page 39 Losevsky Pavel; Page 41 Matt Bien; Page 42 Alexander Motrenko; Page 43 Matt Bien; Page 44 Matt Bien; Page 45 JupiterImages; Page 47 Matt Bien; Page 51 Matt Bien.

Note to Readers: Please note that every effort was made to include accurate Web site addresses for kid-friendly resources listed throughout this book. However, Web site content and addresses change often and the author and publisher of this book cannot be held accountable for any inappropriate material that may appear on these Web sites. In the interest of keeping your on-line exploration safe and appropriate, we strongly suggest that all Internet searches be conducted under the supervision of a parent or other trusted adult.

Printed in the United States of America

Bang PKG 10 9 8 7 6 5 4 3 2 1

This book printed on acid-free paper.

CONTENTS

Welcome to the World of the Game Designer!

Firing lasers, defeating muscle-bound monsters, scoring high points, and winning the game. It's just another day at the office for computer game designers. You already know that playing video games is fun. But what's it like to actually create one? Is designing computer games really as fun as it sounds?

There's no doubt about it: Game design is a creative and exciting field. But (you knew there'd be a "but" didn't you?) it also takes a lot of hard work to take a game from an idea that pops into your head while eating breakfast to a multi-million-dollar product for sale at stores throughout the world.

Game design is a lot like moviemaking—it combines a wide range of different skills and talents. Artists draw and animate the characters. Writers develop the story lines and scripts. Audio engineers record the sound effects and put in the music. Programmers build the software and computer codes that make the games run. Designers themselves often know a little bit about all these things, and they come from very diverse backgrounds. Some started as animators; some were game testers; some were even hockey players as you'll discover in one of the interviews included in chapter five.

The one thing all game designers want is to make a good game that players will enjoy so much that they keep coming back for more. The trick is that the game can't be too hard and it can't be too easy. "Good video games are long, complex, and difficult," says James Paul Gee, author of the book *What Video Games Have to Teach Us About Learning and Literacy*. "But if children couldn't figure out how to play them, and have fun doing so, game designers would soon go out of business."

Do you have what it takes to be a game designer? Play around with the idea a bit. Read this book, do the activities, take the quizzes, and find out what it's really like to be a computer game designer. Who knows? You could someday become one of the top scorers in the game biz.

Imagine a job where you play computer games all day long!

CHAPTER 1

Get Ready for Action

FIND OUT MORE

What will they think about us 100 years from now when an archaeologist discovers one of today's most popular video games? Pretend you are there a century from now and describe people's reactions. What do computer games say about our current culture?

You've found it at last: Buried under a wild tangle of vines, the ancient temple of Thurl still stands as a crumbling monument to a long-lost civilization. It is also the lair of Ja-Krill, leader of a race of evil lemur-men you have sworn to destroy...before they destroy you! The mossy stones echo as you climb the temple steps with your only remaining weapons—a double-edged thunder ax and the magical amulet of Vir, which helped restore your health after your nearly fatal battle with the vampire monkeys. A twig snaps behind you, and suddenly a massive purple-clawed beast hurtles out of the undergrowth, aiming for your throat! But your reflexes are swift, and the thunder ax finds its mark. As the hideous beast crumples at your feet, a glowing message appears in the air above your head: CONGRATULATIONS! GO TO THE NEXT LEVEL.

This fantastic otherworld of danger and excitement is the brainchild of a person called a game designer, who imagined it all—every vicious boss monster, every dancing cactus and super-strength-giving mushroom, every possible strategy and even the smallest detail associated with the weird fantasy realm you immerse yourself in every day when you get home from school.

"I think a **video game** is **all** about articulating a dream."
—MARK MEADOWS, ARTIST, WRITER, AND GAME DEVELOPER

As game designer Mark Meadows says, "I think a video game is all about articulating a dream."

Think getting paid to play games all day and conjure up fantastic scenarios like this one sounds like the most awesome career on earth? A lot of game designers would agree with you, but they

Some of your favorite board games have gone high-tech.

Tomb Raider is a popular computer game that inspired a movie.

would also say that they work really hard at what they do, logging in long hours at the computer screen. Let's find out what it's *really* like to dream up another world and make it a reality.

Ancient Gamers

The need of human beings to challenge themselves by playing games might be nearly as basic as their need for food, shelter, and sleep. Archaeologists have unearthed artifacts of games such as Mancala, a 3,500-year-old game that originated in ancient Africa—which you can still find on the shelves of many toy stores—and something called "the Royal Game of Ur" because no one knows what the Sumerians who actually played the game 4,500 years ago called it. The Egyptian board game of Senet, a version of which people still play today, was popular as far back as 2,600 B.C.

Games, which fulfill an important social function in our development, have grown and evolved along with human culture. In fact, as many sociologists will tell you, you can learn a lot about a culture by looking at the games people like to play. Today's high-tech computer games have more in common with ancient board games than you might expect. Many electronic games, such as Sid Meier's Civilization (voted the number-one best game of all time by *Computer Gaming World* magazine), are based on board games, with the difference that the computer rather than a second player serves as the opponent.

The Game That Started It All

Electronic games developed along with computers, increasing in speed and complexity in step with rapidly evolving technologies. The great-granddaddy of all today's computer games was called Spacewar!, developed in 1961 by Steve Russell, a Massachusetts Institute of Technology (MIT) student, whose nickname was "Slug." In Russell's two-player game, each person maneuvers a spaceship and fires missiles at the other player's ship while trying to avoid the gravitational pull of the sun. Spacewar! ran on a computer the size of a vending machine that cost $120,000 but had only 4k of memory. (In 2006, most handheld game consoles cost about $100 and feature 2,000 times more memory!) Spacewar! was the world's first fully interactive video game, and it caused a huge sensation at MIT's annual Science Open House in 1962.

Fast forward to the next millennium! Computer games recently celebrated their 40th birthday. Who knew in 1962 that in just a few decades they would explode into a multibillion-dollar industry, which would one day surpass movie box-office receipts? In fact, some of the people who developed the first electronic games didn't even bother to copyright their designs. To get an idea of how important video games have become, consider this: Video games and movies were once seen as two entirely separate forms of entertainment. Then came video games whose characters and plots were adapted for movies such as *Tomb Raider: The Movie*, *Mortal Kombat*, and *Resident Evil*.

Gaming Visionaries

The history of video game design is a story of individuals who were able to imagine fantastic possibilities and then, with creativity and patience, make those fantasies real. People like Ralph Baer, a young engineer who wondered why a television couldn't have a game built into it. Or Nolan Bushnell, who spent a summer working in a carnival arcade and began to dream of a whole arcade filled with computer games. Bushnell went on to design an arcade version of Spacewar! called Computer Space, which debuted in 1970. Then Bushnell helped start the first video game company, called Atari, which is Japanese for "check" in the game of Go. In 1972, Atari came out with Pong, essentially an electronic ping-pong game. Players used "paddles" (small bars on each side of the screen) to bat a tiny ball back and forth until somebody missed. Pong was incredibly simple...and incredibly addictive. When Atari market-tested the game at a local bar, the owner called to complain that the coin slot was jammed with quarters

CHECK IT OUT

Civilization is a single-player turn-based strategy game in which the objective is to build an empire from the ground up. The most recent version of this game, Civilization IV, came out in late 2005.

because so many people wanted to play the machine! In 1978, Atari introduced Space Invaders, an arcade game with a new feature: It displayed the highest score, tempting players to try and beat it. Space Invaders was so popular it caused coin shortages in Japan, and in the U.S. kids were skipping school to play the game —not that you would ever do anything so foolhardy, of course!

Gurus of Game Design

Atari is just one of the companies that would help shape game design history. Japanese companies like Nintendo (which can be translated as "Leave luck to heaven") and Sony also had a huge impact on this business. Japanese game designer Shigeru Miyamoto created a game for Nintendo called Donkey Kong, which featured a hero named Mario, who spawned a massively successful family of related games. Gamemaster Shigeru, long considered

Gamemaster Shigeru Miyamoto with Mario, one of his famous game world heroes.

"Video games are **bad for you?** That's what they said about rock and roll."

—MASTER GAME DESIGNER SHIGERU MIYAMOTO

one of the top designers in his field, is also the creative force behind Nintendo's Legend of Zelda series. Other highly respected game designers include Peter Molyneaux (Populous), Sid Meier (Civilization), John Romero (Doom and Quake), Roberta Williams (King's Quest), Hironobu Sakaguchi (Final Fantasy), and Will Wright (The Sims). As most game designers will tell you, a good computer game should be easy to learn but difficult to master. Updated versions of classic games like Pong, Pac-Man, and Frogger have become popular with a new generation of gamers, proving that a well-designed game will continue to attract players.

Virtual Violence

As video games became more popular, some people began to worry about the violence they frequently depict. A 1975 game called Death Race 2000 , based on a movie of the same name, was taken off the market because the public objected to how the player earned points—by running over stick-figure people. Some have argued that video games encourage violent behavior. In 2003 lawmakers in the state of Washington passed a regulation prohibiting anyone from selling or renting video games to minors in which police officers become targets. In response to a 1993 Senate investigation into video game violence, the Entertainment Software Rating Board (ESRB) was established. The ESRB reviews computer games and assigns a rating to help consumers make informed choices. In 2005 a new rating was introduced: E10+. This rating, for kids ten and up, helps regulate the gap between games rated appropriate for everyone and those for teens.

Game designers know that the potential for interactive entertainment is enormous, and many are convinced that video games

FUN FACTOID

In 1981, a man playing the game Berserk died of a heart attack—the first and only known fatality caused by a video game.

Do Your Games Rate?

Electronic games are rated by the Entertainment Software Rating Board (ESRB) (go to http://www.esrb.org). Each rating has two components: an age-appropriateness rating and a description of content that allows consumers to screen out specific elements they might consider offensive, such as animated blood, crude humor, gambling, etc. Round up all the video games in your house (if you have older siblings, this may take some time!) and make a tally of how many of each rating you find. Look for the rating printed on the front of each cartridge. Because the rating system is a voluntary one, some games are unrated. If you don't have any video games at home, you can look through the collection at a local video store. Some of the ratings you may find include:

FIND OUT MORE

> EC = Early Childhood. Titles rated EC have content that may be suitable for persons ages three and older. Titles in this category contain no material that parents would find inappropriate.

> E = Everyone. Titles rated E have content that may be suitable for persons ages six and older. Titles in this category may contain minimal violence, some comic mischief, and/or mild language.

> E10+ = Everyone 10+. Titles rated E10+ have content that may be suitable for ages 10 and older. Titles in this category may contain more cartoon, fantasy, or mild violence, mild language, and/or minimal suggestive themes.

> T = Teen. Titles rated T have content that may be suitable for persons ages 13 and older. Titles in this category may contain violent content, mild or strong language, and/or suggestive themes.

> M = Mature. Titles rated M have content that may be suitable for persons ages 17 and older. Titles in this category may contain mature sexual themes, more intense violence, and/or strong language.

Do you think the game rating system is useful? Why or why not?

will eventually tell stories as well as, if not better than, movies do. If you want to make your mark in this field, you'll need to start thinking about new ways to make games fun and exciting without relying on the same old violent clichés.

Video Game Mythbusters

Recent studies have shown that certain stereotypes about gamers—for instance, that most of them are pimple-ridden, antisocial teenaged boys—are not actually true. More girls are playing video games than was previously thought (one study shows that

43 percent of gamers are female), and according to MIT professor Henry Jenkins, women now slightly outnumber men playing Web-based games. There are certainly a lot of powerful female characters, such as Lara Croft, battling it out in game land. You might also be surprised to hear that the average gamer is about 30 years old! Though many people worry that playing video games is a solitary activity that isolates players, most kids play electronic games in a social setting, when they get together with their friends, either at home or in gaming arcades, to check out the latest version of Burnout. And the latest MMORPGs (massively-multiplayer online role-playing games) allow thousands of gamers to play together online at the same time!

Mastering the Art of Fun

The increasing dominance of electronic gaming in the entertainment industry suggests that this field has a robust future as long as it continues to satisfy the human hunger for novel forms of fantasy and new challenges. Game designers thrive in environments that draw upon all areas of human culture to constantly redefine the meaning of fun. As Paolo Malabuyo, lead designer for Microsoft's Xbox, reminds us, "As a game designer, in the end what you're responsible for is: Is it fun or not?"

POP QUIZ

True or false?
The rise of video games has led to an increase in youth violence.

A: False. Juvenile violent crime rates in the United States are currently at a 30-year low. There is no proven connection between playing violent video games and behaving violently in real life.

Game Designer at Work

It may seem too good to be true, but getting lots of experience playing games is one of the best ways to prepare for a career in computer game design. Game designers have generally put in long hours in front of computer screens and TV sets, clenching the game controls, building up oversized thumbs and hand-eye coordination that is super-hero fast.

You may think, "This sounds a lot like me. I'm a game freak too. Where do I sign up?"

While only genuine game fans need apply for jobs like these, it also requires some serious know-how to design awesome computer games that kids like you will want to play. It's not enough to enjoy playing games; game designers must also understand *why* games are fun. What makes one game totally irresistible and another a complete flop? What makes them better, faster, more exciting? Is it more fun to shoot 50 fireballs into a troll's stomach and have him keep attacking, or would it be more satisfying to have him explode after three hits? These are the types of heavy questions game designers must ponder on a daily basis.

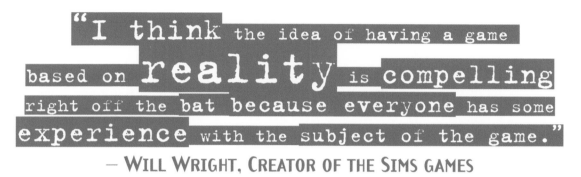

"I think the idea of having a game based on **reality** is compelling right off the bat because everyone has some experience with the subject of the game."

— WILL WRIGHT, CREATOR OF THE SIMS GAMES

A creative office environment keeps the ideas flowing.

In Search of the Next Smashing Idea

Typically, game designers have plenty of firsthand knowledge of games. They know Super Mario Brothers, Doom, The Sims, Myst, and many, many others. They also have experience playing all different types of games, from racecar driving and basketball simulations to alien shoot-em-ups and strategy games. To get new ideas, game designers typically surround themselves with all the playful trappings of pop culture—since, after all, games need to be fun. Walk into a game designer's office and you're likely to find it cluttered with DVDs of adventure movies, science-fiction posters, stacks of comic books, action figures lining the shelves, toy robots, and squeezable rubber heads. In addition to a video game library that would make any game-lover drool with envy, a game designer's office might also come equipped with a pinball machine and a Ping-Pong table, along with Nerf footballs and mini-basketballs for tossing around. As fun as all these games and toys sound there really is a serious reason for having them around: to inspire designers to think creatively. Sometimes, the designers

Keeping track of all the details is a challenge for computer game designers.

16

leave the office to find inspiration—going to amusement parks, zoos, and museums all in search of new gaming ideas.

Successful game ideas can come from almost anywhere. They are often action scenarios, such as prison breaks, car chases, and battles with aliens, androids, and zombies. Games can be based on movies (games about King Kong, James Bond, and other film characters fill the shelves), or they may even come from plain-old, boring, daily life. When The Sims first came out, the game was revolutionary because the characters in the game simply go through everyday activities, like getting the mail or going to the movies. Few thought it would be a hit, but The Sims became one of the biggest-selling games of all time—mostly because it captured the imagination of nontraditional gamers.

Usually, when designers hit on an exciting possible game idea, they have to dig a little deeper and do some research to accurately develop it. If they're creating a game about capturing dinosaurs, they'll want to study the different prehistoric beasts: What do they look like? How do they run, eat, and attack? What sounds might they make? If they're developing a game about Vikings, they need to know: What kind of clothes did they wear? What types of weapons did they use? What did their ships look like? Details are the name of this game. Designers work hard to make the situations in their games as authentic as possible.

Ideas for Sale!

So what do you do if you have a great idea and all the skills you need to create the next bestselling computer game? First, you want to outline the premise and basically get your vision on paper so you can "pitch," or sell, your idea to a game publisher. You may work internally at a company for a game publisher or you may work externally, as an independent freelancer. Either way, you will need to pitch your ideas in the same way that directors and writers pitch their movie ideas to producers. You often need one sentence that captures the essence of the game—that's known in the game biz as the "high concept." If your game is about outer space knights who happen to look like deer, your high concept might be "It's *Star Wars* Meets *Bambi*."

Once you grab the interest of a publisher with your "pitch," you may need a more developed written outline of the story,

Imagine This!
How creative are you? Take an ordinary object (like a colander or a rubber glove) and take a few minutes to brainstorm ten new ways to use it. Wacky and weird ideas are just as welcome as practical, functional ones.

sketches of the characters, and then storyboards that go through the basic plot. Storyboards are used in the movie industry, too. They look like giant comic strips, and they illustrate and outline the main action of the video game.

Your ultimate goal is to convince the publisher that the game will sell, and a storyboard describing the action lets others see what you are envisioning in your very creative mind. Sometimes some basic game business knowledge will help. You might need to show how much it would cost to develop the whole game and a timeline for completion.

A Typical Day in Game Land

Once you've sold your concept, it's time to get to work! Imagine your life as a game designer, and you will see it's different from the average office job. You start your day by slipping on one of your gaming uniforms—either a T-shirt and jeans or a sweatshirt and khakis. As you head off to the office on the freeway or subway, you probably don't look like part of the average suit-and-tie-wearing crowd. Let's face it: It's hard for you to get the creative juices flowing when you're formally dressed. You have to feel comfortable, playful, and creative.

You start the day meeting with other game designers, graphic artists, and audio experts to update each other and discuss how your work is going. Your *game producer* leads the meeting, going around the room asking each team member for a progress report on how things are coming along. After the morning meeting, it's back to the "drawing board," which is really your computer monitor where you probably spend 90 percent of your time creating the real details of your game.

You have been working on an idea of ogres running amok in a castle, but you now need to get into the nitty-gritty. You think of the goals for the players. You've been debating: Should the player knock down as many as ogres as possible and finally capture the thimble of lightning or should the player avoid as many ogres as possible while climbing up several levels of a "beanstalk" and then finally grab the golden goose? It's a simple detail but the right execution can make or break a game.

To hash over some ideas, you take a break and invite the graphic artist to go to the company game room with you for a

round of Ping-Pong. As you play, you loosen up and describe your lead character and the other characters that the players will encounter, such as the "boss monsters" that appear at the conclusion of each level of the game. Still not quite sure what to do, you head over to the local art museum hoping to find some inspiration.

Browsing through an exhibit of ancient Egyptian artifacts, you suddenly have a brainstorm! Your characters will be goofy cartoons instead of very human-looking warriors. You run back to your computer and design a hero who gains more power by opening treasure chests filled with delicious nuclear eggs. He accesses different weapons in different rooms. You add these details to your storyboards and the new ideas really help the flow of the action. When your storyboards are totally done they will give a frame-by-frame rendering of the action that will take place in each scene in the game.

Along the way, you are always thinking of something called the I/O *structure*. I/O is short for the input and output. The input is how the player will use controls to create the action on screen and the output is the graphic images and sounds that the player sees and hears from the gaming platform, whether it's a computer or gaming console.

As you add detail to the storyboards, you also put your ideas into a *game document* or *design document*, which will essentially be a reference guide to every aspect of the game—the overall concept, the outline of the plot, the mission or goals, sketches of characters, obstacles to overcome, and other details. The design document goes over the levels of difficulty and what players need to do to make it to each level. The document can get very elaborate because today's games are so complex.

Many Talents Collide and Come Together

You have already been working closely with a team of artists who are helping refine the look of your characters and building the settings where the action takes place. Today, you still have a couple hours left, so you visit with the sound designer to discuss what the ogres will sound like when they howl, punch, and fall. You also review ideas for the music that will be used in different scenes. As elements in the game develop, you must keep track of

CHECK IT OUT

Want to explore careers in game design? Here are two good sites to check out:

Game Design (http://www .gamedesign.net)

Game Jobs (http:// www.gamejobs.com)

all the changes in the design document and make sure everyone on the team is aware of the changes.

Although you depend on a team of specialists, it helps to know a little about everything so you can understand all the components that go into building a game. Game design brings together storytelling, art, programming, and business all in one project.

You may create characters, backgrounds, and other items in a game. To do so, you begin to shape your ideas with traditional pencil and paper. Then you refine your vision on the computer using the latest graphic art and animation software. If you're working on a big game, you depend on graphic artists who know exactly how to conjure up the amazing characters and fantasy worlds.

You turn to programmers to make the game actually work, but some designers take on this job as well. Programmers write the lines of code that tell the computer how the game should operate. When you push a button, the programming code can tell a character to get a weapon, jump super-high, scale a wall, or capture an opponent.

If you are the lead designer in a big game company, you may be heading a group of other game designers called *level designers*. Level designers work with tools called *level editors* or programs that let them take elements created by the art department and place them easily in a game. The graphic artists may have created trapdoors, giant hammers, boss monsters, or mountains—obstacles that the hero must deal with. Using a level editor, the level designers easily place them where they want in the game. Entire days can be devoted to just the backgrounds—forests, kingdoms, and outer-space landscapes all take time to produce. Level designers focus on creating a game level or mission. In a way, level designers are like bricklayers and graphic artists are like brick makers.

Bugs and Glitches

When the game is close to completion, game testers are brought in to give it a try. Game testers are often young game-playing fans who will play the game over and over, taking notes along the way about any problems (called bugs) and things they like and dislike about the game. If you're a designer, you pay close attention

FUN FACTOID

The game industry is seasonal, with the biggest sales at Christmas. Statistics show that about 50 percent of the game industry revenues come from pre-Christmas sales. Games don't sell as well during the summer when people are enjoying themselves outdoors. The interesting exception is for sports games, which people tend to buy during the season of the particular sport.

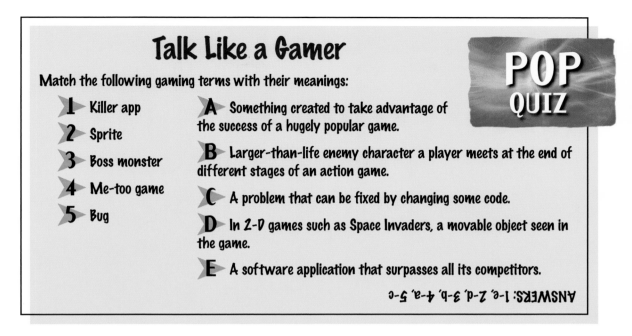

Talk Like a Gamer

POP QUIZ

Match the following gaming terms with their meanings:

1 Killer app

2 Sprite

3 Boss monster

4 Me-too game

5 Bug

A Something created to take advantage of the success of a hugely popular game.

B Larger-than-life enemy character a player meets at the end of different stages of an action game.

C A problem that can be fixed by changing some code.

D In 2-D games such as Space Invaders, a movable object seen in the game.

E A software application that surpasses all its competitors.

ANSWERS: 1-e, 2-d, 3-b, 4-a, 5-c

to their comments and make changes based on their evaluation. If the game always crashes at a certain point, the designer will want to consult with the programmers and correct the code that is causing the problem. Often game designers start out as game testers—because testers usually have a real passion about video game play.

Going Gold

After the three to twelve months—or longer—that goes into creating a game, a designer can relax—a little bit—when the game is finally being manufactured. Those in the business say that at this stage the game is "going gold." Then, the designer just has to worry about sales. If your game doesn't sell, you won't get the chance to make more games. That's why designers often consult with the marketing team at a game company. Marketers are the people who help package and sell the product. Marketers need to know about all the qualities that will make your game appealing to players so they can advertise those special features.

Game Design Tech and Trends

Electronic games have come a long way from 1975 when Pong—basically a computerized version of tennis—was the rage. Pong by Atari really launched the computer game craze, first as electronic arcade games and then as a game you could play on your home TV through a new invention called the *game console*. Quickly on the heels of Pong arrived more sophisticated games like Asteroids, Space Invaders, Centipede, and Pac-Man. Interestingly enough, just as video games seemed to be taking off, they fizzled out for a while during what's known as the Great Video Game Crash of 1983-1984. Arcade business dropped off, and home systems weren't generating sales. But in 1985, the Nintendo Entertainment System (NES) breathed new life into electronic games with Super Mario Brothers. After the NES, new game consoles came along like the popular PlayStation from Sony and Xbox from Microsoft.

As consoles developed, so did player controllers. What started with a simple joystick evolved into an elaborate range of buttons and special features. Certain games today use light guns that let you blast directly at your TV screen, bringing down your enemies with a ray of light.

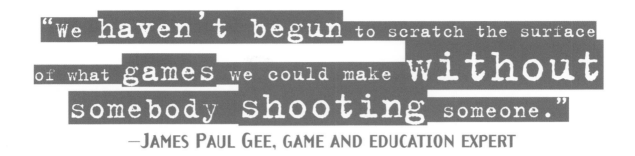

"We haven't begun to scratch the surface of what games we could make without somebody shooting someone."
—JAMES PAUL GEE, GAME AND EDUCATION EXPERT

A special "force-feedback steering wheel" makes playing current racing games more realistic by responding to road conditions (you feel vibrations when you veer off the track and hit a bumpy patch). Combine that with stereo surround sound, and you can feel like an actual NASCAR racer. Dance Dance Revolution, which started as a very popular arcade game, is keeping people

Computer gamers flock to expos like this to see all the new technology.

Computerized games can be played on all kinds of gadgets.

on their toes at home as well. Instead of using standard controls, you interact using an electronic dance mat that connects to your home console. You get points for your timing and correct steps as you try to duplicate the onscreen dance moves and cues.

The Personal Computer Revolution

In the 1990s, computers became more affordable and user-friendly, and CD-ROM drives became a standard component. With both IBM PCs and Apple Macs equipped with these drives—plus lots of memory—games in a CD format took off. Manufacturing, packaging, and distributing games on compact disks was and still is incredibly affordable.

Now with high-speed Internet connections, a new type of computer game play has been catching on fast, where people can log on and play with large numbers of other players. Called massively-multiplayer online role-playing games, or MMORPGs, these online worlds are in progress when you sign in and they keep going after you log out. You typically pay a fee to play on-line as much as your heart desires (and your parents will allow!).

Lineage, a subscription-based game with 10 million registered users, can be simultaneously accessed by 100,000 players all over the world.

High-speed Internet has also made it possible to purchase and download games as well. As technology improves, you'll be able to buy bigger and better games direct over the Internet and download them to your computer's hard drive.

Fun on the Run: Meet the Gadgets

We live in a world that is constantly on the move, so it's only natural that gamers wanted their fun to go as well. At the same time that electronic games were bursting into arcades and home consoles, manufacturers were introducing handheld video game devices. Mattel was one of the pioneers with simple handheld LED (light-emitting diode) football and baseball games. Milton Bradley then produced a handheld console with interchangeable mini-cartridges so you could play different games on one device. Other handheld game gizmos followed, but it took a while to get the formula right.

Then in 1989, Nintendo unveiled the GameBoy, invented by Gunpei Yokoi. The graphics weren't flashy, but the device was cheap and the games–like Tetris–were fun. Over the past decade, the games have improved dramatically with color graphics and a wide range of game choices. GameBoy has gone on to become the most successful game system ever, selling more than 100 million units worldwide.

When it comes to electronics, consumers often have a Swiss Army-knife mentality: They want a device that does it all. So it only seemed natural to combine electronic games with personal digital assistants (PDAs) and mobile phones. Some phones double as cameras, after all–why not add in a game feature? Mobile phone companies are offering games that users can buy and download into their phones. The 2005 Digital Gaming in America study by Ziff Davis showed that more and more people are engaged in cell phone gaming and that the average cell phone gamer spent $13 a month on games. Advances in technology are also allowing people to compete in real-time against other cell phone gamers.

The lowdown on downloads: You can download lots of free games at http://www.download-games-online.com.

Advances Behind the Scenes

Game designers not only have to keep up with all the new ways games are being played, but they also have to learn all the new software and programming tools that can make their job easier. Some of the new technologies coming down the pike are nothing short of amazing.

People thought it was pretty cool when ten years or so ago, designers created characters strictly for 2-D environments where players moved up and down, right and left. An increase in chip speed and memory has allowed games to become much more complicated and fast moving, and the animation has become very sophisticated. The two-dimensional "sprites" that scooted around the screen in an early game like Asteroids look very crude when compared to the incredibly realistic 3D characters that populate a game like Final Fantasy, for instance. These characters are built from scratch starting with polygons and then fleshed out with shadows, textures, lines, and colors.

As sophisticated as that technology may be it pales a bit next to a new technology called *motion capture*. This technique captures the live motion of a human being and then converts that motion into data that can be viewed as a 3-D image in a game. While it is especially used in sports games, you see it more and more in all sorts of new games. Actors are now used for many motion capture sequences. Tiny pads are attached to their bodies—arms, legs, torso, and head—to record precise movements and map them in the computer where they are used to animate game characters.

The Future

Virtual reality that fully plunges players into another world is coming soon to computer games. Inventors have already developed virtual reality visors that let you see and feel everything in a 3-D environment. If you turn your head left, you see what's left in your virtual environment. The visor is used in conjunction with virtual reality gloves that let you make gestures and interact with the virtual world merely by moving your hands. If you see a can of soda in your virtual reality visor, you can just reach out with your hand, grab it, and pour it in a cup. Some of this technology is already available for home use, but expect to see it more commonly used in the years ahead.

CHECK IT OUT

The PBS show *The Video Game Revolution* offers a fascinating look into the history of electronic gaming. You can visit the program's Web site (http://www.pbs.org/videogamerevolution), which features games to play and a great interactive timeline of gaming history.

Virtual reality is the wave of the future in computer games.

Artificial intelligence (AI) is another area that is advancing rapidly, making characters more complex and realistic. AI is the programming that lets the characters you encounter in a game respond with diverse motions and possibilities. The enemies you face in games like Medal of Honor: Allied Assault and Half Life really put players to the test because the AI is so good.

Current Shifts in the Game-o-sphere

Computer games are always changing. And they are changing the way we live, too. The following are trends to keep on your screen:

Emotional Rescue. If video games are ever to truly rival movies as a medium for telling stories, they'll need to inspire a wider variety of feelings and responses in their audience. Some designers believe that the future of games will be in the realm of the emotions—they want to increase the range of feelings a game can in-

"I wanted a different way in which to tell my stories. Coming up with concepts for computer games gives me another avenue of creative expression."

—TOM CLANCY, BEST-SELLING AUTHOR AND FOUNDER OF RED STORM ENTERTAINMENT

spire in a player, and which a player can express in a game. Considering how hard many gamers have fallen for Lara Croft, this trend doesn't sound so unlikely! Games featuring virtual pets, such as Tomaguchi or Nintendogs, already encourage players to become emotionally attached to the creatures they care for. The director Steven Spielberg thinks games will really have matured "when somebody confesses that they cried at Level 17."

She's Got Game. If it's true, as research seems to show, that playing video games teaches important problem-solving and reaction skills, then girls are being shortchanged by an industry that still caters primarily to male gamers. Lots of people in the gaming biz see female gamers as a huge untapped market, but many video games designed for girls tend to promote stereotypical interests such as makeup and fashion. What makes a computer game female-friendly? Girls generally prefer games requiring cooperation and which emphasize problem solving and strategizing. If you're serious about working in the game design field, here are some things you can do, according to Janese Swanson, Ed.D., to design electronic games that girls will want to play

• Create characters that both girls and boys enjoy. Avoid stereotypes and myths about females and males.

• Create products and marketing strategies that feature healthy female role models.

CHECK IT OUT

Great sites for girl gamers include http://www .girltech.com, http:// www.girlstart.com, and http://www .smartgirl.org.

• Have girls test products and offer their opinions on all aspects of a game, from color to content.

• Create ads and packaging for your product that feature girls actively participating in and enjoying the use of technology.

Serious Play. Video games aren't just for entertainment. Game technology is used to train soldiers, businesspeople, and medical professionals as well as airline pilots and space shuttle astronauts. Hazmat: Hotzone uses tools from the world of electronic gaming to create a powerful training tool for firefighters who tackle hazardous emergencies such as chemical spills or terrorist attacks involving biological weapons. Gaming technologies are also being used in classrooms to help students like you master skills and information. Kar2ouche (by Immersive Education company) lets students recreate scenes from Shakespeare's plays. Other games address social and political emergencies around the world: Peacemaker is an interactive simulation game that allows Israeli and Palestinian teenagers to explore strategies for peaceful coexistence; Escape from ObeezCity addresses the problem of obesity in children.

Super Mario Next to Mona Lisa? Computer game animation has become so refined that people now treat game images like high art. A Los Angeles gallery show called "Into the Pixel" displayed 16 of the best images taken from new games. The Whitney Museum of American Art in New York, the San Francisco Museum of Modern Art, and the Massachusetts Museum of Contemporary Art all have mounted shows examining the influence of video games. Serious artists are under the game spell as well. Painter Greg Simkins's recent work shows Pac-Man as ailing and old—way past his dot-eating prime.

Any way you look at it—past, present, or future—computer gaming is a fun business to work in. It's creative, cutting-edge, and full of challenges. And who knows where it will go next?

Game Designer in Training

There are many ways to work up to the level of game designer. Some people begin as game testers. Some enjoy programming. Others are artists or animators. The one thing they all have in common? They would all rather be playing games than just about anything else in the world, and they typically know a little bit about a lot of things—from computer programming to story writing to graphic arts.

Playing a lot is probably the most important education a future game designer can have. Can you imagine telling your parents that you're going to do nothing but play games in college? "How do you expect me to be a successful designer, Mom, if I don't play Madden Football all day?" Good luck with that conversation!

Becoming a designer means more than just play, though. You also have to study what you play, and you can start doing that now. Begin your education by taking notes about games. Ask yourself: What works best? What features don't quite cut it? What makes them fun? What would you do to improve them? Think why you lose and win at a game. Think what the rewards are—do you get more ammunition, gold, or power as you advance? Or do you simply complete a puzzle? Keep a

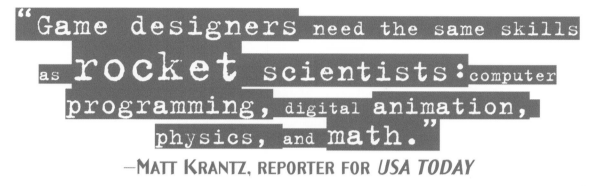

"**Game designers** need the same skills as **rocket** scientists: computer **programming**, digital **animation**, physics, and **math**."

—MATT KRANTZ, REPORTER FOR *USA TODAY*

notebook of your thoughts, and it will help you in developing your own games. Also, play as many different kinds of games as you can to see the variety out there.

Getting a game made requires leadership, organization, and teamwork—talents you can develop while in school by joining

Video games provide a next-best-thing-to-being-there experience.

Future game designers should plan on taking lots of computer classes.

a group. By participating in a band, a sports team, the school newspaper, a church group, or scouting, you can gain the experience of completing a project with others. If you help produce your school yearbook, for example, you will definitely see what it takes to organize a project, coordinate with others, meet a schedule, and work with a budget.

Tap into Your Creative Spirit

The game universe combines the two worlds of creativity and technology. It's an interesting mix of freethinking and precision. On the creative side, the most important skill may be the ability to tell a good story. You might be able to think up characters for a game, but you have to write out what they will do, what their motivations are, and what their overall mission is. You need to think how to build suspense and conflict. Games need plot and structure, and a sense of plot will help you outline your entire game idea with all its different scenes, levels, backgrounds, and characters. On the technology side, you need the technical know-how to make the creativity come alive online.

The director Steven Spielberg, who is starting to get into the game-making business and developing three original games with video game maker Electronic Arts, told students at the University of Southern California that the game industry needs to improve the storytelling, character development, and emotional content just as it has enhanced the images and action.

English and writing classes can teach you how to be a strong story writer, and the written and oral communication skills you learn in these classes will help you when pitching ideas to publishers, explaining your vision to the creative team, and writing instruction manuals.

Because games attract players with their vivid characters, fantastic backgrounds, and dynamic animation, lessons in art certainly can aid the budding designer. Designers need to sketch out characters, costumes, weapons, buildings, and more. Knowledge of graphic arts programs can really be useful. As you advance in your education, try to gain experience with programs such as Adobe Photoshop and Illustrator. Also, courses in animation will help you bring exciting action sequences to life. Eventually, try to get some practice using common animation software such as Studio Max or Flash.

Master Computer Basics

Computer technology not only brings your artistic vision to life, but it really is the foundation on which this whole business is built. So you really should learn as much as you can about game software and programming. Remember, misplace one line of computer code and an entire game might shut down. Programming codes let players communicate with the computer to instruct characters how to move. Common programming languages used in the

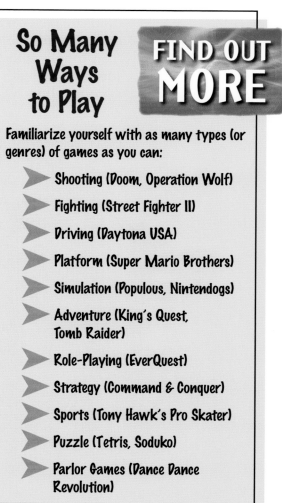

So Many Ways to Play

FIND OUT MORE

Familiarize yourself with as many types (or genres) of games as you can:

➤ Shooting (Doom, Operation Wolf)

➤ Fighting (Street Fighter II)

➤ Driving (Daytona USA)

➤ Platform (Super Mario Brothers)

➤ Simulation (Populous, Nintendogs)

➤ Adventure (King's Quest, Tomb Raider)

➤ Role-Playing (EverQuest)

➤ Strategy (Command & Conquer)

➤ Sports (Tony Hawk's Pro Skater)

➤ Puzzle (Tetris, Soduko)

➤ Parlor Games (Dance Dance Revolution)

gaming business are Visual C + + and C, which students often learn about in high school or college. For Web-based games and games on small electronics like cell phones, Java programming is typically used.

Before you even learn programming though, you can take math courses in high school that will help you understand programming concepts, such as algebra, geometry, trigonometry, and calculus. More advanced courses would be in data structure, 3-D mathematics, and algorithms.

A "math brain" comes in handy for figuring out different action sequences. Say 500 angry monsters are charging at your hero and you have an automatic sling shot that flings 50 stones a minute. You need to realistically figure out how many monsters you can topple with this type of weapon. Every character's actions depend on math and science. If your hero flips a heavy sumo wrestler, how high will he fly in the air and where will he land?

Let the games begin!

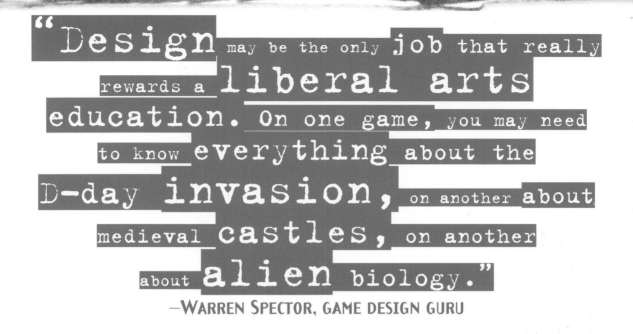

"Design may be the only job that really rewards a liberal arts education. On one game, you may need to know everything about the D-day invasion, on another about medieval castles, on another about alien biology."

—WARREN SPECTOR, GAME DESIGN GURU

The laws of gravity and motion are in play, so some basic physics knowledge will make this action sequence realistic.

History courses can help game designers, too. How people lived, the way they dressed, the homes they lived in, the cities they built can all fuel ideas. Corey Dangel, an art director from Microsoft Games Studio, says that people with musical backgrounds, dancers, and actors, tend to make strong animators and designers because they understand how bodies move and react. It's really amazing how diverse the educational backgrounds of designers can be.

Earn a Gaming Degree

As the gaming industry has grown, however, designers increasingly need very specific skills. That's why several colleges now offer associate and bachelor's degrees in video game design. While four-year colleges will give you a broader background of knowledge and hold more prestige than two-year schools, two-year programs will teach you the nuts and bolts and, obviously, take less time and cost less. It's a toss-up. You'll have to decide whether more education is a better choice for you or, if you'd rather get out there creating games and learning on-the job. Edu-

Art directors help put all the ideas and images together.

cation can always help you advance by equipping you with new skills, but ultimately how you perform at work will be the key to advancing.

Typical courses include game production, visual design, interactive storytelling, and the business of gaming. Some courses stress interface design, which is the relationship between the buttons that the player uses and the characters in the game world. Other classes focus on AI (artificial intelligence), which is the programming that tells the on-screen characters how to act and react according to what the player does. Courses often combine classroom study with lab time that gives students hands-on experience. Many of these colleges offer internships as well, which are a great way to learn on the job and find possible employment.

Schools such as Full Sail in Winter Park, Florida, and DigiPen in Redmond, Washington, specialize in teaching computer game design. A handful of colleges, including the University of Baltimore, the Georgia Institute of Technology, and Carnegie Mellon, currently offer graduate degrees in this field. Given the growing success of the computer game industry, more are sure to follow.

A goal for many of the graduates from these programs is to compile samples of their design work on a CD-ROM that they can send to potential employers. The CD-ROM is a portfolio or a sampling of a graduate's best work that shows a range of style and capabilities. The CD-ROM portfolio should show that they can animate, create, and manipulate a variety of 2-D and 3-D images. Some will demonstrate that they can make a change to an existing game (called a *modification* or simply a *mod*).

If you're starting to seriously consider game design as a career, explore the different colleges that offer game design as a major. And really dedicate yourself to studying the business in your spare time—visit game Web sites and blogs, read game magazines, and try to talk to people who are in the industry now. They can tell you firsthand what type of training you need and how to break into the field.

Draw It!

Game designers need to create storyboards to illustrate their ideas, so having some artistic talent is a requirement in this job. Find five everyday objects to sketch with a pencil—then show your sketch to a friend or family member. If they can identify each of your drawings, you've got some talent. If they turn your sketch upside down and tell you it's a nice picture of mashed potatoes, it's time to head back to the drawing board.

CHAPTER 5

The "Players" Who Bring Games to Life

You don't have to be a designer to blast into a career in the game industry. Although designers get the credit and fame for thinking up a game, other professionals join in the process. Some of these other careers may better suit your talents and personality. Check out these related jobs:

Game Tester

A common way that young people break into the industry is by becoming a game tester. If you're at least 18 years old and have a love of games, you can sometimes find part-time work testing when a game is in development. While it may seem like a dream job to play games and get paid for it, testers have to be very critical and pay close attention to what they think is fun or not. As part of a company's quality assurance (QA), testers are often asked to take notes about what they find easy, challenging, or too hard. Testers keep a log of all the things that don't work right or make sense. They are on constant lookout for "bugs," or problems in the software that cause the game to behave strangely. Game publishers may videotape the screen action during a test so that when a mistake happens, they can easily rewind and find the glitch. Publishers also welcome any constructive ideas testers might have on how to improve the game.

FUN FACTOID

Jeremy "Jez" San, head of Argonaut Games, started his own company when he was 16 years old!

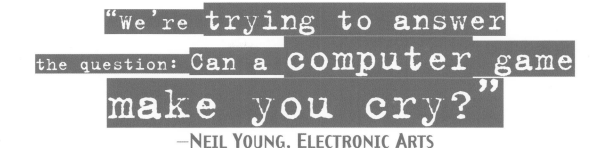

"We're trying to answer the question: Can a computer game make you cry?"

—NEIL YOUNG, ELECTRONIC ARTS

Computer game testers know that a game's ultimate success is all in the details.

A related part of game testing is *configuration testing*. A configuration tester tries out a game on a variety of consoles to make sure it works with different equipment.

Publisher

Publishers are the bosses and owners of the big and small companies that make the games and get them into the stores. Publishers

NAME: Dawn Boughton

OFFICIAL TITLE: Executive Producer

What do you do?

I produce Internet games for Disney Channel, Mattel, Nickelodeon, and other clients. We make games to promote TV shows like *Dora the Explorer*, *Kim Possible*, and *Avatar*. The games are all based on Flash, a common Web animation software. Most of the games are for young kids, a fun audience.

My primary role is to be organized and get the project done on schedule and budget. I'm also the main communicator between the client and the game team. Plus, I oversee all the content and say, "Is this fun? Can we do this? Is it easy to play?"

I'm focused on usability. You have to make a game that's intuitive to play especially for a young audience on the Internet. They don't want to read directions; they want to log on and have fun. All games need to be challenging, though—that's where the fun is.

I love my job! I get to make super-fun games and I'm always learning new technologies for the Web. It's constant creativity and growth.

How did you get started?

When I was growing up, I played Nintendo, but I wasn't passionate about games. As it turns out, though, I was a producer all along. In high school, I was stage-managing plays. When I went to Evergreen State College for experimental film and animation, I gravitated toward producing projects for my classmates. I was always organizing projects, and it took me a while to realize that producing was a natural talent for me.

I taught myself Flash and how to build Web sites. I started at Smashing Ideas as an animator when the company was about eight people, and now I am a producer and there are 45 people working here. It's a boys' world right now in gaming, but don't let that hold you back—more women are getting involved.

are in charge of financing, manufacturing, marketing, and distributing. They oversee the whole operation from printing of the boxes and instruction booklets to the purchase of TV, Internet, and magazine ads. They come up with a business plan for the entire company and all financial success or loss typically rests on their shoulders. Since they are the ones with the money to fund new products, they are also the ones with the power to say yes or no to a new game idea.

Marketer

The best game in the world will never be a hit unless the people know about it. That's the job of marketers. They are specialists at getting attention through publicity and advertising. Whether they are typing a persuasive press release or are on the phone telling the media about a new product, marketers rely on strong communication skills. When a game is first being launched, they're in charge of setting up any events that introduce it to the public. They also decide how advertisements should look and then place ads in magazines and newspapers, on television, the radio, and the Web. Marketers frequently have a say in the box design as well because they want to make sure it is something that will grab the buyer's attention.

Sound Designer

Crashes, crunches, bells, grunts, roars—every sound blaring from your screen has to be coordinated and produced by a sound designer. These audio engineers do work that is similar to regular recording engineers who make CDs. Using microphones, computers, mixing boards, and other audio equipment, they know the basics of recording and editing sounds. A lot of the work

"I dream for a living."
—STEVEN SPIELBERG, MOVIE DIRECTOR
AND COMPUTER GAME PRODUCER

Getting the sound right is what sound designers add to the mix.

involves putting sound effects in the games. Musical scores for games have evolved from simple repetitive sounds to more elaborate full soundtracks. Sound designers may even record dialogue with real actors. Famous actors such as Jack Black and Charlize Theron have contributed their voice talents to video games.

Composer

Computer game music has become so elaborate that people make careers composing it. The soundtrack for the game Metal Gear Solid 2 was written by Harry Gregson-Williams, who scored dozens of films, including *Shrek* and *Armageddon*. As in the movie business, game composers make music that matches many scenes and moods, from uplifting and victorious to dark and threatening. The music is unique because it has to change as rapidly as a player's performance. If you win over a long stretch, the music has to keep changing to match what's happening on screen.

NAME: Ken Kato
OFFICIAL TITLE: Audio Design Manager

What do you do?

I design how an entire game sounds. It's challenging because you have to think how the sounds will behave according to what the players are doing. I record and mix soundtrack music, voice-over acting, and sound effects. We use a mixture of pre-recorded sound effects, and then we spend time and money on getting unique sounds. For example, the racing game Project Gotham features racetracks in various parts of the world, so we went to Italy, England, Germany, and Spain. We stood in street corners with headphones, microphones, and recorders and captured the specific city ambience.

Another fun part of my job is that we get to break things. When we were working on the racing game Forza, we set up a junk car and used a forklift to pick it up and drop it from 10 feet high. We smashed the windows with sledgehammers, and recorded it all. We then edited the sounds in the studio, sweetened them up, and you hear those crash sounds as part of the game.

We also make a lot of trips to grocery stores to buy fruits, vegetables, and meat products. We go through them and squish and crunch items to make really gloppy, gross sounds. One of the funniest things we did was with my toy fox terrier. She's a tiny five-pound dog that fits in my pocket. When you wave your hands in front of her face, she starts growling. We recorded that and pitched it down quite a bit and it sounds really nasty. That's one of our monster sounds.

How did you get started?

I was a music major in college with an emphasis in recording science. I studied digital audio recording and I played keyboard, which is very helpful on this job. After college, I got a job in multimedia production and I was soon working for Microsoft. My advice to any young person who wants to do this is learn the tools. Find out about the audio engineering equipment and software that are used in today's studios.

NAME: Jennifer Boespflug

OFFICIAL TITLE: Software Test Lead

What do you do?

I test computer games that are played on the Internet and on Xbox. I first worked on family Internet games such as checkers, cribbage, bridge, and chess. Later, I worked on games for Xbox, including Nightcaster, Tork, Project Awesome Racing III, and a cute game called Psychonauts [www.psychonauts.com] about a boy who has psychic super powers and goes to psychic camp. I run what are called "build verification tests (bvts)," which make sure all the functions of a game work. So I have to pay close attention to every detail.

ON THE JOB

When I was little, I really liked the magazine *Highlights*. The magazine always had a puzzle where you had to find how many different things were wrong with a picture. That's what game testing is like. You have to find the upside down umbrella in a game. You have to find the bugs or problems. Some of the bugs aren't too exciting. A lot of times the games just crash.

My advice to kids: Don't get into videogames because you think it's easy and just sitting on the couch playing. You have

to care about engineering and software and detail and methodology. Also, I would love to see more women get interested in this career. We need more creative, wily people in this industry.

How did you get started?

We had computer labs in our elementary school and I loved playing computer games. We had an Atari and Nintendo at home but I never considered video games as a career. I was interested in environmental policy and that's what I studied in college. While in school, I joined a computer users group, learned some programming, and loved it so much that I couldn't stop doing it. I started teaching how to build Web sites and helped optimize databases on campus just for fun.

When I graduated I was heading toward an environmental policy job, but my friends encouraged me to send my resume to a few tech companies. I immediately had several amazing offers on the table. One offer was to be a test engineer in the Internet gaming zone at Microsoft. I had no idea what testing was. I decided to try it as a temporary tester and within a year I was offered a permanent position.

Graphic Artist/Animator

Although a designer can be the graphic artist as well, often a large game company employs artists who are dedicated to creating the characters, backgrounds, and other elements—whether it's a race course, a dank tunnel, or a landscape with shrubs, craters, and gravel. Besides having an education in drawing, painting, and other traditional techniques, artists need to master the latest graphics programs. While 2-D (two-dimensional) painting and animation skills are still essential, 3-D modeling and 3-D animation are more the norm in the best-selling games. These characters are typically built using "wire frames" that you see on your computer screen. The artist constructs the character on this frame, layering it with skin and clothes. These layers are called *textures*. And the characters don't just run right and left. They maneuver through elaborate 3-D rooms. They can have subtle motions like a chest that steadily rises and falls as they breathe. They can even sweat! For detailed backgrounds, artists may use a technique called *tiling*. If a scene requires rain, tiling lets you create a square of how you want the rain to look. Then you can take that "tile" of rain and simply paste it through your background as needed.

Graphic artists use their talents to bring the characters and backgrounds to life.

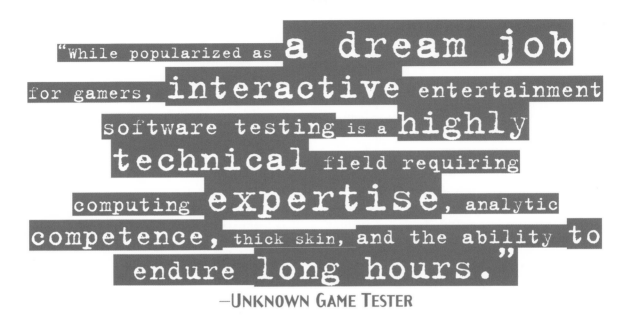

"While popularized as **a dream job** for gamers, **interactive** entertainment software testing is a **highly technical** field requiring computing **expertise**, analytic **competence**, thick skin, and the ability **to endure long hours.**"

—UNKNOWN GAME TESTER

CHECK IT OUT

It takes a village to create a game. Open the manual for any PlayStation 2 game and check out the credits page to get a sense of how many people it takes to put out a video game.

Technical Writer

While designers write the creative stories for games, technical writers draw on precision, organization, and logic to produce all the practical guides that help others use and produce the games. After trying the game repeatedly, technical writers churn out the manuals that explain how to play, the rules, limits, and rewards. Sometimes, they write the help screens on Web sites for players who have questions.

Scriptwriter

Just like major motion pictures, hit games are only as good as their scripts. The scriptwriter makes a document detailing all the visual action and the audio. Designer and audio engineers follow the script to make sure all the sound and visual elements are in place for the completed product.

Game Reviewer

The game industry has exploded to such a level that being an official game reviewer is a real career option. These are the writers who try out games and write about what they like and dislike in the various game publications. Pop culture and music magazines, as well as newspapers, all hire game reviewers.

NAME: Travis Kotzebue

OFFICIAL TITLE: Artist/Animator

What do you do?

I do 2-D design that includes storyboards, character concept art, environment concept art, traditional 2-D animation, and a lot of Flash animation for game scenes and Web site stuff. I created a number of villains and supporting characters in the Sly Cooper games. To create a character it's a good starting point to have a reference, such as an actor or real person, so you have set personality traits to play with. Or, sometimes you want an "archetype" of a person. For instance, a nerdy brainy character will look and act much differently from a powerhouse thug who's not too bright. You want to find that personality early on, to give yourself as much to play with it as you can. Then, in the Sly universe, anyway, you want to brainstorm what kind of animal would best personify that personality. Then you just start drawing! I go through tons of unsuccessful sketches before finding something workable. Tons and tons. It's all about refining what works and throwing out what doesn't. Ninety-nine percent of the time another artist will scrutinize the design and catch something you haven't thought of, and add ideas that make the character work better. That's the most awesome part of collaboration because the end result is always so much better.

Game design is an intense world though, and you really have to keep up with other artists who are on top of their game, so you have to put your best work out there every day.

How did you get started?

I never set out to work in games. I'm a comic guy really. A total fanboy. I started doing Flash work for Web site animations and games right out of school. I did that for a couple years, then moved to children's CD-ROM games. The working artist community is kind of small enough that you all get to know each other. So through some of my buddies I'd made at various companies, I moved on to other game projects.

Pressure Cooker

How well do you handle pressure? A video game publisher may invest millions of dollars toward a game's development, and a game design that tanks in the marketplace can lose millions, so there's a lot riding on the game-making team. If you've ever played any sports, you probably know whether or not you tend to choke when the pressure is on. If the thought of having to perform under these conditions makes your palms start to sweat, do yourself a favor and choose a less stressful career!

Producer

Every project needs a leader. And in the game industry, producers are the grand pooh-bahs. (The only person higher up than a producer is the publisher who owns the whole company.) Producers oversee each project, including the schedule, the marketing, and the distribution. They hire, fire, and inspire their staff. The job requires amazing organizational skills. Controlling the budget may preoccupy producers most. Today's games can cost millions of dollars, and publishers expect producers to keep costs down. These professionals push their team of designers, artists, programmers, and testers to complete their work on deadline, so they can get games manufactured and earning money. To help their workers to do their jobs and reach their "milestones," producers act as cheerleaders, boosting team spirit as the work intensifies. Producers also look for new talent and game ideas. If they think a great new game might be based on a popular movie or book, producers get all the right permission and licensing to use that material, which is usually another expense.

Localization Producer

This is a unique career in which you make sure that versions of games are appropriate for each country in which it is distributed. Is all text and dialogue translated? Are elements in the game understandable by the culture? A reference to July 4th fireworks makes sense in America but not in Japan. Changes are often made for versions of games in each country.

Programmer

The programmer is the techno-whiz who really brings the game to life. He or she gives the game a brain so when you push a button, a character will leap, or when you move a lever, the hero will run down a hallway screaming. While game designers really should know some programming basics, these professionals are the experts. They write lines of code that make the whole game act and react. Programmers usually fall into different categories. There are *engine programmers* who write the programming that is the basis for the entire game. There are *tools programmers* who develop the scripting tools and level editors that the designers use to build the game. *Artificial Intelligence (AI) programmers* write the rules of behavior so the computerized characters can make intelligent actions based on any situation. If you try to swing a sword at a character's knees, he should try to jump high. If you shoot a laser at him, maybe he dives behind a nearby sofa for protection. The code tells the character that if you do "A," then "B" is his best option. Programmers pay close attention to comments from the game testers—if there's a problem, the code is usually to blame.

This is truly a massively multiplayer industry that relies on people doing all these jobs and many others. If you are obsessed with games, there is sure to be a profession that matches your unique talents.

CHAPTER 6

Kids Ask, Game Designers Answer

To find out what kids really wanted to know about being a computer game designer, we went to the source and asked real middle school students from Illinois, California, and New York for questions they would ask real game designers. We presented the questions to Dean Richards, designer of NHL hockey games for Electronic Arts, and Hal Milton, lead game designer at SONY Online Entertainment. Here's what they said:

Did you play computer games as a kid and what inspired you to become a video game designer?

–Sophie M., age 9, New York, New York

Dean: I grew up playing sports all my life and I ended up leaving college early to play hockey professionally in Europe. Because of the kind of lifestyle I led, I had a lot of free time to play video games. I enjoyed video games so much that when I finished my career playing hockey, I took a digital media arts class and learned Web building and different art and design programs like Photoshop. I really got into it, and I really enjoyed animation. Computers and technology just really interested me. I thought I'd like to work for EA sports as an animator. I applied to become a game tester first to get inside and see all the possibilities before I made the decision to follow that career path.

I started as a tester on a soccer game and then got moved over to hockey where I became a designer.

Hal: My mom says that when I was 13, I was playing Ultima 3, and my folks had people over for a dinner party, and I walked out and announced to everybody, "I know what I'm going to do for the rest of my life. I'm going to make video games." My father said, "Well, you got to do, what you got to do."

Still I wound up going to college for a degree in radio, television, and film. I did a little bit of film work, but I really didn't like it. I decided to join the game industry because it tends to be a much more collaborative field. Artists, designers, and developers really work together and you get to dip your hands into all aspects of the work.

To get my foot in the door, I started as a game tester, and then offered my services as a sound designer, game designer, and writer.

Hal Milton

What type of research do you have to do before designing a game?

—Christopher G., age 10, Chicago, Illinois

Dean Richards

Dean: My hockey game comes out every year so I have to know the current teams and current players. All the NHL teams are on the game, as well as the Swedish, Finnish, Czech, and German European Leagues. Things change in the sport every year, and I have to keep up to date. The NHL had new rules to open up the game this year. I had to put that into our game. We are trying to be authentic. We make sure the real players are represented in the game. Jaromir Jagr is on the Rangers right now so his face is on that character, and he plays like the real Jaromir Jagr. Because Jagr is a good stick handler, we have made our Jagr a more accurate shot than other players. Our version of Jagr is real hard to knock off the puck just like in real life. When you're playing with the superstars in our game, they actually feel like the superstars. That's part of our game development. We had a player complain that he wasn't fast enough in the game, and we had a good laugh about that and then we made him a little faster the next year.

Hal: You do research into the time period you want the game to be set in. You research how the people lived. Look at how cities were laid out; how people went about their daily lives. With the game I'm currently working on, we had a level where we wanted to create a really high tech office resort building—something spectacular that you could see a super villain living in. For an exotic location, we thought let's find a tropical island that we really liked so we picked some islands off of Thailand. We gathered all these photos of Thailand for reference. Then we said what's the best coolest looking building we can find. The Burj Al Arab tower in Dubai is this amazing structure with these huge helipads that come off the top of it and beautiful arcing sail-like shapes. We took that building and we took that Thai island and we combined the two and then applied our own ideas on top of them. We made our own unique vision.

Do you enjoy your job and if so why?

—Francesca V., Age 10, San Carlos, California

Dean: Yes. I love being creative and working in a fun environment. I also love hockey and I get to talk about hockey strategy at work. That's my job. Most people would love to do that. I go to lots of games and I review hockey game tapes. That's one of the greatest things about being here.

Hal: I enjoy working with others and taking something from my head and putting it onto the screen. Sometimes, people think you're crazy when you say you have a great idea like: the monkeys will just pick up the ray gun and make the crane fall down and free all the chickens. Everyone laughs at first, but you draw the mechanics for how it works and you convince the guys to build it. It's an amazing feeling. Working with people and sharing the results of your labor are the most rewarding moments I've ever had.

Brian S.

What is the hardest part of designing a game?

—Leo L., Age 10, Chicago, Illinois

Dean: You're always looking for that "wow" factor year to year. You want to come up with that one feature that is going to be innovative that is just going to blow people away. For example, when we introduced a play called the "one-timer," that really changed the way you play. A "one-timer" is a game play where you make a pass, and you don't need to get control of your puck to shoot it. As soon as it hits your stick, you can release it. Before you had to get control of it, then shoot, which took too much time.

Hal: The hardest part of game design is accepting the fact that you're never right the first time. It takes lots of tries to get an idea to work as you originally think it should. When a

Jackson G.

project gets killed—that's a very hard part, too. The last game I worked on was killed about a year before it was going to ship and I had worked on it for three years. The company was trying to cut costs and decided to kill the project. That's part of the business and it's heartbreaking. All of us were reduced to tears.

What is your favorite game that you designed?

—Brian S., Age 10, Chicago, Illinois

Dean: NHL, of course.

Hal: Ultima Online and Wing Commander. They're both old games but they're great.

What makes a successful video game?

—Jackson G., Age 10, Chicago, Illinois

Dean: We make sure it's fast and you have good scoring chances. We appeal to a built-in hockey-fan audience, but we also want to reach out to non-hockey fans and show them that playing hockey is fun.

Hal: No one man makes a successful game—it's a team effort. A number of the games I make are massively multi-player games (so the players input makes these games). I never anticipated the number of regular people who have such a deep understanding of what I'm working on. A lot of these people have become experts on the games. These fans have tight, large communities that organize their thoughts online and discuss the games. It's a real communal experience.

Is there anything someone my age can do now that would help prepare for a job in computer games?

—Sophie M., age 9, New York, New York

Dean: Developing of a game is like a team sport so if you have that experience it can help. On my team, we have 50 people—artists, audio people, software engineers, and more. We have to gel as a team and really work together to get our game made. Also, if you're good at games and into designing, look at the many different books out there that show you how to do simple programming and see if you like it.

Hal: Play lots of video games and read a lot. And write as much as you can. Half the battle in designing games is being able to state your idea from beginning to end. Theater experience is actually great because you learn how groups have to organize their time and work together. Being in a band would also help. Each person has their instrument but if they don't work together it sounds like garbage. You have to be able to talk to your friends, fight with them and still be friends afterward. You have to stand up for your ideas and accept other ideas when they're right—and that all takes lots of practice. If you love to tinker and hack into things, that can be one of the best lessons. If you're serious about exploring, a whole lot of games now come with editors, especially for the PC. A full editor lets you use all the assets in a game to create your own adventures. Really detailed ones, too. It's incredible.

CHAPTER 7

Virtual Apprentice

COMPUTER GAME DESIGNER FOR A DAY

Ready to take the Virtual Apprentice challenge and be a computer game designer for a day? Here's a timeline you can follow on your own, or you can ask your teacher to make this a multi-player role-playing activity.

8:00 Game On: Brainstorm! Take a blank sheet of paper and make a list of the most preposterous game titles you can think of, the sillier the better! This is especially fun to do as a group, because you can spur each other on to new heights of zaniness. (The creators of SpongeBob SquarePants and Teenage Mutant Ninja Turtles probably came up with the ideas for their characters the same way.) When you come up with a title you especially like—The Attack of the Fifty-Foot Thumbs!—let it serve as your inspiration for the work that follows.

9:00 Create a killer concept statement that sums up what your game is all about in the oh-so-cool and very memorable statement. "It's *King Kong* meets *Iron Chef*" Or "Think 3-D chess while bungee-jumping!"

10:00 Start working on storyboards using pictures cut from magazines, printed from the Internet, or sketched by hand using colored pencils or markers. Storyboards, which are like cartoons that show a sequence of frames, are used in the movie and the gaming industry to illustrate what the action in a scene should look like. Draw a storyboard (3-4 frames or so) of an exciting scene from the game you're developing.

11:00 More storyboarding—this is your chance to make a big splash. Take the time to make yours spectacular.

12:00 Fish sticks for lunch—you need to feed your brain!

1:00 When you walk into a video game arcade, the first thing that hits you is the NOISE, right? You've created some great eye-grabbing images—now it's time to start thinking about how you want your video game to sound. Experiment making all kinds of different noises, using your body or various objects you find around the house or the classroom. Try to come up with at least five unusual, ear-catching sounds to accompany the visual action of your game.

2:00 Put together a game-design portfolio. Artists such as illustrators and photographers display their best work in a portfolio to impress potential employers. Label a binder or file folder with your name, and your home address or the name of your school. Your portfolio should feature a short description of the game concept you've developed for this assignment along with the storyboards you created. You can also include samples of any artwork or drawings you've done that you're especially proud of along with descriptions of any puzzles and games you've invented (or plan to invent someday!).

3:00 Time to balance all the brainwork with a physical workout. Go play a game in the real world, something that gets your body moving and your heart racing! Don't forget to exercise your thumbs by playing a round of a favorite video game or two.

4:00 Pitch your product to your parents, friends, or classmates as if they were the publishers of a big electronic games company with lots of money to spend on developing your game. Listen carefully to their feedback. Are they ready to fork over the big bucks to make your game happen?

5:00 Heave a big sigh of relief now that the presentation is over. Based on your "publisher's" reaction to your idea, come up with a list of five things you need to do next. If they rejected your game concept, what can you do to refine your ideas and present a better pitch? If they loved your game, what do you need to do to get your game ready for prime time?

If you can meet these challenges and come up with an idea for a great new game that will virtually blow the competition out of the water...maybe the next big game guru could be you!

Virtual Apprentice
GAME DESIGNER FOR A DAY: FIELD REPORT

If this is your book, use the space below to jot down a few notes about your Virtual Apprentice experience (or use a blank sheet of paper if this book doesn't belong to you). What did you do? What was it like? How did you do with each activity? Don't be stingy with the details!

8:00 BRAINSTORM:_____

_____

_____

_____

9:00 CONCEPT STATEMENT:_____

_____

_____

_____

10:00 STORYBOARDS: _____

_____

_____

_____

11:00 MORE STORYBOARDS:_____

_____

_____

_____

12:00 LUNCH: _____

_____

_____

1:00 SOUND EFFECTS: _____

_____

_____

_____

2:00 GAME DESIGN PORTFOLIO: _____

_____

_____

_____

3:00 WORKOUT: _____

_____

_____

_____

4:00 PRODUCT PITCH: _____

_____

_____

_____

5:00 WHAT'S NEXT LIST: _____

_____

_____

_____

Count Me In (or Out)

ARE YOU GAME?

The following questions may help you find out if you're ready to rock the video game world with your amazing new game designs. Mark your answers on a separate piece of paper and refer back to them when you reach the next level.

If given the choice to do one of the following activities for a whole day, I'd choose

❑ Going for the championship in a favorite outdoor sport.

❑ Hanging out with a few friends to play video games.

❑ Shopping till I drop at the local mall.

❑ Curling up on the couch with a good book or the TV remote control.

Video gaming is my life and I can't think of a better way to make a living than designing computer games. Someday I'd like to create games that:

_____

_____

_____

_____

Video games are cool but instead of designing them I think I'd rather work in the background doing something like:

_____

_____

_____

_____

Video games are OK to play, but when it comes to a future career I'd rather:

_____

_____

_____

_____

I can't imagine a more perfect job for me! The next step in my game plan for the future is to:

_____

_____

_____

_____

After reading about the Great Video Game Crash of 1983-1984, I've decided to use my technological know-how in a profession that isn't so risky—like

❑ Nuclear energy.

❑ Robotic housecleaning.

❑ Dandelion-fueled tugboats.

Whether I design them or someone else does, a few game ideas I'd like to play around with are:

_____

_____

_____

_____

_____

_____

APPENDIX

More Resources for Game Designers

BOOKS

Gerardi, Dave and Peter Suciu. *Careers in the Computer Game Industry*. New York: Rosen Publishing Group, 2005.

Sheff, David and Andy Eddy. *Game Over: Press Start to Continue*. Wilton, Conn.: Cyberactive Media Group, 1999.

Lund, Bill. *Getting Ready for a Career as a Video Game Designer*. Mankato, Minn.: Capstone Press, 1997.

Oleksy, Walter. *Video Game Designer*. New York: Rosen Publishing Group, 2000.

PROFESSIONAL ASSOCIATIONS

International Game Developers Association (IGDA)
870 Market St., Suite 1181
San Francisco, California 94102-3002
http://www.igda.org

WEB SITES

There are a gazillion great sites chock full of information about game design. Here are a few places to start:

A virtual tour of Game On, the video game exhibit at the Museum of Science and Industry in Chicago:
http://www.msichicago.org/gameon/index.html

Other fun gaming sites include:
http://games.zeeks.com/games.php
http://www.headbone.com
http://www.indiegames.com

You can learn more about animation at:
http://www.animationarena.com
http://www.alice.org

You can learn more about game programming at:
http://www.gameprogrammer.com/gpwiki

Two helpful sources for game industry career info:
http://www.gamasutra.com
http://www.gamedev.net

INDEX